Hamburgers
Plain and Fancy

Hamburgers Plain and Fancy

by CEIL DYER

Publishers   GROSSET & DUNLAP   New York

Introduction

The inspiration for this book came to me while in France. I had just returned to Paris from a two week gastronomic tour of the Provinces, and there I sat at a sidewalk cafe, sipping my apéritif and waiting for my omelette aux fines herbes. The city was as beautiful as ever, my apéritif was delicious and I knew that my omelette would be, as always, exceptionally good, but all of a sudden, I was homesick. I longed to be back in the United States. But most of all I wanted a hamburger, an honest to goodness U. S. hamburger on a U. S. hamburger bun with mustard and pickle, and a slice of tomato, and French fries of course, with ketchup for dunking. Or a cheeseburger, perhaps, with onion and sharp Wisconsin cheese, or with chili—a Texas red hot —or a California burger supreme. I closed my eyes and could almost smell the fragrant aroma of hamburgers cooking on a California patio grill.

Why can't you get a really good hamburger in Paris,

I wondered? At any small cafe you can order a superb omelette. But "Le Hamburger?" With the exception of one or two places (Le Drugstore or the Plaza Athenée Grill) it does not exist. French waiters look aghast if one is requested; the bakers of France refuse to master the art of the hamburger roll; French chefs look down their noses at any dish not invented in France, and that was my answer of course, the French simply had not been first to think up this particular combination of ground meat and bread. They actually deny its existence—because of professional jealousy. It's true, though no Frenchman will ever admit it. But that in a word is why hamburgers in France are ignored.

Really, I mused, it's rather too bad, the French are after all such wonderful cooks, and the ingredients for a hamburger in the right hands can result in such true gourmet fare.

Juicy meat, brown and crisp on the outside, pink and moist within; lightly toasted roll; just the right amount of onion, relish and pickle—delicious—simply great. Poems could be composed on such food, songs could be sung, recipes should be gathered, books should be written. Books written? I got out my notebook and pen.

Though it is extremely unlikely that an American waiter will ever say, "Here lady, the herb (as in Herbert) burger," with the same flair as his French counterpart when exclaiming, "Voila madame, l'omelette aux fines herbes!", it is hoped that this book will contribute to the elimination of "just hamburgers," and that it will also help to elevate the American hamburger to its rightful place high on the list of all the simple, yet perfect gourmet foods.

Contents

7

Hamburgers Plain and Fancy

1

All About Hamburgers

Gourmet food, say the French, is simply a matter of care and caring. Care in selecting the raw ingredients, in blending and in seasoning, and in caring enough to give that little extra time it takes to cook the perfect dish. So it is with hamburgers.

To make gourmet hamburgers, start by buying the best possible meat you can afford from a reputable butcher you trust. Have it ground to order while you watch. Or better yet take it home and grind it yourself, just before it is to be cooked. With one of the new, preferably electric, grinders it's an easy, almost effortless chore.

Ground meat is extremely perishable; if allowed to remain for too long a time before cooking, juices will be lost and it will become dry and tasteless. Buy ground meat the same day it is to be cooked. If this is not possible, form meat into patties and freeze. Place waxed paper between each patty, stack and wrap in foil, or place in a plastic bag. Hamburger patties will stay fresh in the freezing compartment of your refrigerator up to one week, or they may safely remain in your home freezer for two to three months. (They may be cooked frozen. Contrary to popular opinion, there is no difference in flavor between fresh cooked and frozen cooked meat.)

If you buy already ground meat—and there is virtue in economy—make sure it is a bright pink color all the way through. If it is a dullish gray or there is even the slightest touch of brownish color, do not buy it—it is not fresh. If it is pale pink—too much fat, not enough lean—it is a poor buy at any price. The fat will sizzle away leaving you with less meat than you paid for, and what's worse, a dry and tasteless hamburger.

The best cuts for grinding are: *Boned chuck;* juicy and flavorful, it is more expensive than hamburger but there is less shrinkage when cooking. *Ground round steak;* lean but great tasting, especially when you have your butcher add a little ground suet (about two ounces per pound), or you may add fat in the form of cream or sour cream (approximately two tablespoons to the pound). *Sirloin;* superb. Its only fault is its price, but for special occasions, why not? The resulting hamburger, for real fans thereof, is well worth the additional cost.

How much meat will you need? It depends on your appetite and that of your guests. A pound of ground meat will make two to three superburgers, four large, or six average (but rather thin) hamburger patties.

To make juicy light hamburgers handle the meat as little as possible. The best method to our way of thinking, is to place the meat in a large mixing bowl, sprinkle seasoning and any other added ingredients evenly over entire surface then mix and toss with a fork until well blended. Turn out, and with a light hand, quickly divide and shape into the desired number of patties.

Cooking instructions. Do not flatten meat with spatula or knife while cooking or it will become tough and tasteless. Turn only once. *Broil* three inches from medium high heat. *Grill* over hot coals (never a briskly burning fire). *Pan fry* in a lightly greased or buttered pre-heated heavy skillet over medium heat. *Pan fry in salt:* Cover bottom of heavy skillet completely with salt. Place over very high heat for five to eight minutes before adding meat. Cook over high heat, turning only once, to desired degree of doneness.

Using one pound of meat for four burgers, cook one and one-half to two minutes each side for rare (very pink inside), two and one-half to three minutes per side for medium rare (slightly pink inside). Well done? Don't—the hamburgers will be tasteless no matter what meat is used.

When done to desired degree of rareness, place meat on *warm* rolls. Never, never serve on cold bread.

Split and lightly toast rolls (or oven heat them) the last half minute that the meat cooks. Spread both halves lightly with soft (room temperature) butter before adding meat. Sprinkle meat with additional salt if desired, then top with a little extra butter.

Remember, a hamburger is a *hot* sandwich. Bring *all* ingredients, ketchup, mustard, pickles, tomato slice and onion to room temperature before adding to bun or meat. They should be cold only if they are to be used "with" not "on" as a garnish.

2

Finger Burgers

Rabbit Party Burgers

With Welsh rabbit, crisp pickles, tomato slices and lettuce.

½ small head lettuce	*4 tablespoons ice water*
Welsh rabbit (see page 68)	*8 hamburger rolls*
	Salt
2 pounds ground beef	*Crisp cucumber pickles*

Coarsely chop lettuce. Place welsh rabbit in top half of double boiler over simmering water or in chafing dish to heat.

Mix meat with ice water, shape into eight patties, broil or pan fry. Oven heat rolls. Use long fork to dip each broiled meat patty into hot welsh rabbit, then place on bottom half roll. Sprinkle with salt, add pickles, chopped lettuce and top half of roll.

Eight Burgers

Borscht Burger

With cucumber slices, chopped beets, sour cream, chopped green onion and parsley.

1 small raw beet	*1 pound ground beef*
1 cucumber	*½ teaspoon salt*
2-3 green onions	*1 teaspoon pepper*
½ cup sour cream	*4 hamburger rolls*
½ teaspoon parsley flakes	

Chop beet fine. Peel and cut cucumber into paper thin slices. Chop onion fine; combine with ¼ cup of the sour cream and the parsley flakes. Mix beef with salt, pepper and 2 tablespoons of the sour cream. Shape into four patties. Broil.

Split and toast rolls, spread bottom half of roll with remaining sour cream, add meat patty. Cover with cucumber slices, chopped beets and top half of roll.

Four Burgers

Greek Maiden

With crumbled Feta cheese, chopped fresh mint, sliced red onions and black olive slivers.

¼ pound Feta cheese	*½ teaspoon salt*
6-8 sprigs fresh mint	*2 tablespoons dry white*
1 small red onion	*wine*
6-8 black pitted olives	*Butter*
1 pound ground beef	*4 hamburger rolls*

Crumble cheese, chop mint. Peel and slice onion. Cut olives into slices.

Mix meat with salt and wine. Pan fry in butter.

Split and toast rolls. Spread with soft butter, add meat patty to bottom half. Sprinkle with cheese, mint and olives, add onion slice and top half of roll.

Four Burgers

Dutch Burger

With liver sausage, sauerkraut, caraway seeds and hot mustard.

1 cup sauerkraut (canned)	*2 tablespoons beer*
¼ cup caraway seeds	*4 slices liver sausage*
1 pound ground beef	*1 tablespoon butter*
1 teaspoon black pepper	*4 hamburger rolls*
½ teaspoon salt	*2 tablespoons hot mustard*

Drain sauerkraut and mix with caraway seeds. Place in sauce pan, heat while cooking meat.

Mix beef with salt, pepper and beer. Shape into four patties. Broil. Sauté liver sausage in butter two minutes on each side. Split and toast rolls. Spread with mustard. Place broiled meat patty on each bottom half of roll, cover with sausage, sauerkraut and top half of roll.

Four Burgers

South Boston

With Boston beans, Irish bacon slices, mustard and sweet mixed pickles.

1 small jar sweet mixed pickles
2 cups Boston baked beans
3 pounds ground beef
6 tablespoons Irish whiskey

12 slices Irish bacon
1½ teaspoons salt
12 hamburger rolls
Mustard

Drain and coarsely chop pickles. Place beans in heavy sauce pan over low heat.

Mix meat with whiskey and salt. Shape into twelve patties. Place with bacon on broiler racks. Broil until done to taste.

Split and toast rolls. Spread with mustard, place meat on bottom half. Cover with hot beans, bacon slices, pickles and top half of roll.

Twelve Burgers

Daisy May

With turnip slices, radishes, cucumber, tomato ketchup, cauliflower pickle and parsley.

1 small turnip
4 radishes
1 cucumber
Juice of ½ lemon
½ teaspoon salt
1 pound ground beef
1 teaspoon pepper

½ teaspoon garlic salt
½ teaspoon hickory salt
2 tablespoons ice water
4 pats butter
4 hamburger rolls
4 sprigs parsley
4 cauliflower pickles

Peel and cut turnip, radishes and cucumber into paper thin slices, sprinkle with lemon juice and salt.

Mix together beef, pepper, garlic and hickory salts and ice water. Shape into four patties. Broil.

Oven heat rolls, split. Place a meat patty on each bottom roll, add pat of butter, turnip, radish, cucumber slices and top half of roll. Spear parsley and cauliflower pickles on cocktail picks. Place in center of hamburgers.

Four Burgers

Madison Ave.

With chive cream cheese, walnuts and chopped endive.

1 (3 ounce) package chive cream cheese	*1½ teaspoons pepper*
	1½ teaspoons salt
4 tablespoons butter	*½ teaspoon ground cumin*
½ cup chopped walnuts	*4 tablespoons chili sauce*
2 endives	*2 tablespoons crushed ice*
3 pounds ground beef	*12 hamburger rolls*

Blend chive cream cheese with butter and walnuts. Coarsely chop endive.

Mix meat with pepper, salt, cumin, chili sauce and crushed ice. Shape into twelve patties. Broil.

Split and toast rolls. Spread bottom halves with cheese mixture. Add a meat patty to each, spread meat with remaining cheese mixture. Add chopped endive and top half of roll.

Twelve Burgers

Surf Rider

With pineapple slices sautéed in butter, green pepper and pickled onions.

½ *small green pepper*
8-10 pickled cocktail
   onions
1 pound ground beef
½ *teaspoon salt*
2 tablespoons ice water
4 slices pineapple
   (canned)

1 tablespoon butter
4 hamburger rolls
2 tablespoons butter
   (room temperature)
1 tablespoon mustard

Mince green pepper and onions, combine. Mix meat with salt ice water, and shape into four patties. Broil. While meat broils, sauté pineapple slices in butter over low flame for five minutes. Split and toast rolls, spread with soft butter and mustard. Sprinkle each bottom half with green pepper and onion. Add broiled meat patties and pineapple slices. Cover with top half of roll.

Four Burgers

Susy Wong

With Chinese plum sauce, bean sprouts, chopped radishes and water chestnuts.

8-10 small radishes
1 small can bean sprouts
1 small can water chest-
   nuts
3 pounds ground beef
2 tablespoons ice water

½ *teaspoon salt*
Butter
Soy sauce
12 hamburger rolls
1 bottle Chinese plum
   sauce

Wash, partially peel and chop radishes. Open canned bean sprouts, drain; open canned water chestnuts and cut into thin slices. Combine all three ingredients.

Mix meat with ice water and salt, shape into twelve

patties, pan fry. When done to taste, sprinkle with soy sauce. Split and toast rolls, place a meat patty on each roll bottom, spread with plum sauce, add radish-bean sprout-water chestnut mixture. Cover with top half of roll.

Twelve Burgers

Acapulco

With guacamole, tomato and shredded lettuce.

½ *small head lettuce*	2 *tablespoons ice water*
1 *tomato*	4 *hamburger rolls*
1 *pound ground beef*	1 *cup guacamole**
4-6 *drops Tabasco sauce*	*Salt*
1 *teaspoon Accent*	*Pepper, coarse grind*

Coarsely chop lettuce, cut tomato in half, gently press out seeds and juice and cut into small thin strips. Combine with lettuce.

Mix meat with Tabasco sauce, Accent and water. Shape into four patties. Broil.

Split and toast rolls, spread bottom half with guacamole, add broiled meat patties, sprinkle with salt and coarsely ground black pepper. Cover with lettuce-tomato mixture and top half of roll.

Four Burgers

Pizzaburger

With anchovies, roasted peppers, Mozzarella cheese, stuffed green olives and pizza sauce.

* *See Chapter 5, page 70.*

1 small jar stuffed green
olives

2 green peppers

2 cups pizza sauce*

4-6 drops Tabasco sauce

¼ teaspoon orégano

½ teaspoon coarse ground
black pepper

½ teaspoon salt

3 pounds ground beef

24 thin slices Mozzarella
cheese

12 hamburger rolls

Drain liquid from olives, coarsely chop. Place green peppers on broiler rack as close to heat as possible. Roast, turning frequently, until skins turn black on all sides. Rub off skins. Cut peppers into narrow strips, discarding seeds and fibers. Sprinkle with salt.

Combine pizza sauce, Tabasco sauce, orégano, pepper and salt. Add 6 tablespoons of this sauce to meat. Mix well and shape into twelve patties. Broil.

Heat remaining sauce over low flame. Place Mozzarella cheese slices on split rolls. Toast until cheese is melted and bubbly. Make sure to cover rolls completely with cheese.

Place a broiled meat patty on each roll bottom, cover with hot pizza sauce, roasted pepper slices, chopped olives and top half of roll.

Twelve Burgers

Bombay

With slivered almonds, shredded coconut, chopped onion and mango chutney.

* See Chapter 5, page 79, or use canned sauce.

1 small Bermuda onion
1 pound ground beef
½ teaspoon salt
1 teaspoon pepper
2 tablespoons dry red
  wine
Butter

4 hamburger rolls
2 tablespoons mango
  chutney
2 tablespoons shredded
  coconut
2 tablespoons slivered almonds

Chop onion fine. Mix meat with salt, pepper, and wine. Shape into four patties. Pan fry in butter. Split and toast rolls. Spoon chutney on each roll bottom. Add meat patty, sprinkle with chopped onion, shredded coconut and slivered almonds. Cover with top half of roll.

Four Burgers

Mama Mia

With fried eggplant, Marinara sauce, Provolone cheese and sliced tomatoes.

2 tomatoes
1 small eggplant
2 pounds ground beef
1 teaspoon salt
1 teaspoon coarse ground
  black pepper
2 tablespoons Chianti
  wine

2 tablespoons olive oil
1 clove garlic
1 teaspoon butter
1 cup Marinara sauce*
8 slices Provolone cheese
8 hamburger rolls

Cut tomatoes in eight slices, discarding end pieces. Peel and cut eggplant into eight slices and trim to the same size as hamburger rolls. Mix meat with

* See Chapter 5, page 77, or use canned sauce.

pepper, salt and Chianti wine. Shape into eight patties.

Heat oil with garlic until bubbly in a heavy skillet. Remove garlic. Add eggplant slices. Brown on both sides. Remove, place on large piece of foil, wrap loosely, place in 250° oven while cooking meat.

Pour oil from skillet, wipe clean with absorbent toweling. Add butter, heat to sizzling, add meat patties. Pan fry. When almost done to taste, pour in Marinara sauce. Continue cooking only until sauce is hot. Cover each meat patty with cheese slice. Cover skillet. Let stand one minute to warm cheese. Split and toast rolls. Place eggplant slice on each bottom half of roll. Spoon on a little Marinara sauce. Add patty, additional sauce, tomato slice and top half of roll.

Eight Burgers

Burger Mit

With wilted lettuce, crumbled bacon, mustard and sweet and sour pickles.

½ cup sweet and sour pickles	*1 teaspoon salt*
	½ teaspoon pepper
¼ head Boston lettuce	*2 pounds ground beef*
3 slices bacon	*2 tablespoons ice water*
1 tablespoon tarragon vinegar	*8 hamburger rolls*
	2 tablespoons mustard

Chop pickles fine. Coarsely chop lettuce. Cook bacon in large heavy skillet until crisp, remove and crumble. Pour off all but two tablespoons of bacon grease from pan. Add lettuce, stir-fry until wilted (two-three minutes), add vinegar, crumbled bacon and the salt and pepper. Mix well. Combine meat with remaining salt and pepper and ice water. Shape into eight patties. Broil. Split and toast rolls. Place meat patty on each bottom half, spread meat with mustard. Cover with wilted lettuce, chopped pickles and top half of roll.

Eight Burgers

Angostura Caper

With mayonnaise, minced green onions, Angostura bitters, capers and tomato slices.

1 large tomato	*½ teaspoon salt*
6-8 green onions	*1 teaspoon pepper*
½ cup mayonnaise	*2 tablespoons ice water*
3-4 drops Angostura bit-	*Butter*
ters	*4 hamburger rolls*
1 pound ground beef	*2 tablespoons soft butter*
¼ cup capers	

Cut tomato into four slices, mince green onion. Mix mayonnaise and Angostura bitters together. Mix beef with capers, salt, pepper and ice water. Shape into four patties, broil. Spoon mayonnaise on tomato slices and add to broiler rack for the last three minutes of broiling. Split and toast rolls, spread with butter. Place broiled meat patty on each bottom half. Cover with tomato slice and top half of roll.

Four Burgers

Parisburger

With caviar, chopped chives, French mustard and watercress.

2 pounds ground beef   8 hamburger rolls
¼ cup Burgundy wine   8 teaspoons mustard
1 teaspoon coarse ground   1 small jar caviar
  black pepper   1 small bunch watercress
Butter

Mix meat with wine and pepper. Shape into eight
patties, pan fry in butter. Split and toast rolls, spread
with mustard. Add a patty to bottom half of roll,
sprinkle with caviar, cover with watercress and cover
with top half of roll.

Eight Burgers

Healthy Ham-Burgers

With raw mushrooms, chopped raw spinach, Smithfield ham spread and chopped mixed pickles.

4-6 large mushrooms   1 teaspoon pepper
6-8 fresh spinach leaves   2 tablespoons ice water
½ cup mixed pickles   4 hamburger rolls
1 pound ground beef   1 small jar Smithfield ham
½ teaspoon salt   spread

Cut mushrooms crosswise into thin slices. Coarsely chop
spinach and pickles. Mix meat with salt, pepper and
ice water. Shape into four patties. Broil.

Split and toast rolls, cover with ham spread. Add a
broiled meat patty to each. Cover with mushroom
slices, spinach, pickles and top of roll.

Four Burgers

Old Fashioned

With smoked ham slices, Swiss cheese, garlic butter and crisp cucumber pickles.

4 tablespoons butter
¼ teaspoon garlic salt
2 pounds ground beef
½ teaspoon salt
1 teaspoon pepper
2 tablespoons Bourbon whiskey

8 hamburger rolls
Butter
8 slices Swiss cheese
8 slices cooked smoked ham
24 cucumber pickle slices

Mix butter with garlic salt. Combine meat, salt, pepper and whiskey. Shape into eight patties. Broil. Split rolls, spread with butter, heat in oven. Place cheese slice on each bottom half of roll, cover with broiled meat patty, a ham slice, pickles and top of roll.

Eight Burgers

Yellow Finger

With sliced oranges and Bermuda onion rings marinated in French dressing.

1 large seedless orange
1 Bermuda onion
½ cup French dressing*
2 tablespoons Worcestershire sauce

1 pound ground beef
2 tablespoons ice water
½ teaspoon salt
Butter

Cut orange and onion into paper thin slices, place in non-metal bowl. Cover with French dressing mixed

---

* *See Chapter 5, page 74, or use bottled dressing.*

with Worcestershire sauce. Let stand at room temperature two hours or longer.

Mix meat with ice water and salt. Shape into four patties. Pan fry in butter.

Drain orange and onion slices. Split and toast rolls; spread each roll bottom with soft butter, add meat patty, orange and onion slices. Cover with top half of roll.

Four Burgers

Matador

With Mexican molé sauce, chopped scallions and grated Monterey Jack cheese.

1 small can Mexican molé sauce	*Coarse salt*
¼ lb. Monterey Jack cheese	*2 pounds ground beef*
	4-6 drops Tabasco sauce
4-6 scallions	*2-4 tablespoons ice water*
4-6 radishes	*8 hamburger rolls*

Pour molé sauce into top half of double boiler. Place over simmering water. Grate cheese, coarsely chop scallions and radishes.

Cover bottom of cast iron skillet with coarse salt. Place over high heat. Mix meat with Tabasco sauce and ice water, shape into eight patties. Cook, turning once, until done to taste. Split and toast rolls. Dip each cooked meat patty in hot molé sauce, place on bottom half of roll. Sprinkle with cheese, scallions and radishes. Spoon on any remaining molé sauce and cover with top half of roll.

Eight Burgers

Puckerburger

With lemon and fresh pineapple slices, broiled in butter and brown sugar.

1 lemon	*½ teaspoon salt*
3 tablespoons butter	*2 tablespoons ice water*
4 slices fresh pineapple	*4 hamburger rolls*
1 tablespoon brown sugar	*Salt*
1 pound ground beef	

Cut lemon into paper thin slices, discarding end pieces. Melt butter in heavy frying pan, add lemon slices and pineapple in single layer. Cook over low heat until fruit is soft (about five minutes). Sprinkle with brown sugar. Cover pan and cook until sugar has melted.

    Mix meat with salt and ice water. Shape into four patties. Broil. Split and toast rolls. Spoon melted butter from frying pan on bottom half of each roll. Add meat patties, lemon and pineapple slices and top half of roll.

Four Burgers

Neapolitan

With fresh tomato sauce, Provolone cheese, lettuce and Italian black olives.

2 large ripe tomatoes	*¼ cup sweet Vermouth*
1 tablespoon water	*2 teaspoons salt*
1 tablespoon olive oil	*2 pounds ground beef*
4-6 drops Tabasco sauce	*8 slices Provolone cheese*
1 teaspoon salt	*8 hamburger rolls*
1 teaspoon black pepper	*8 lettuce leaves*
¼ teaspoon orégano	*8 large Italian olives*

To make sauce: Coarsely chop tomatoes, place in a sauce pan with water. Cook, stirring often, until reduced to a thick pulp. Add olive oil, Tabasco sauce, salt, pepper and orégano. Cook, stirring until well blended.

Mix Vermouth and salt with meat, shape into eight patties. Broil. When done to taste, cover with cheese slices. Continue broiling only until cheese starts to melt. Split and toast rolls. Spoon some of the sauce on the bottom half of each roll. Add broiled meat patty, spoon on additional sauce. Top with lettuce. Cover with top half of roll. Spear olive with cocktail pick, place in center of hamburger bun.

Eight Burgers

Alfredo's Burger

With Parmesan cheese, butter, crisp spinach leaves and tomato slices.

½ cup grated Parmesan cheese	3 pounds ground beef
½ cup butter, room temperature	⅓ cup dry red wine
	Butter
1 teaspoon coarse ground black pepper	12 hamburger buns
	12 tomato slices
1 teaspoon salt	Raw spinach leaves

Combine cheese, butter, pepper and salt. Cream to a smooth paste.

Mix beef with wine, shape into twelve patties, pan fry in butter. Split and toast rolls, spread both halves with cheese-butter mixture. Place a broiled meat patty on each bottom half, top with tomato slice and spinach leaf. Cover with top half of roll.

Twelve Burgers

Ah So Burgers

With sweet and sour sauce, broiled peach halves and slivered almonds.

Juice from #2 can of
* peach halves*
¼ cup white wine vinegar
¼ teaspoon ground ginger
2 tablespoons soy sauce
¼ teaspoon salt
¼ teaspoon pepper
1 teaspoon cornstarch

2 tablespoons water
2 pounds ground beef
2 tablespoons ice water
½ teaspoon salt
8 canned peach halves
8 hamburger rolls
½ cup slivered almonds

To make sauce: Combine first six ingredients in sauce pan. Cream cornstarch and water together. Stir into first mixture, bring to boil. Lower heat and allow to simmer for three or four minutes.

Mix meat with ice water and salt, shape into eight patties. Broil. During the last three minutes the meat cooks, add peach halves to broiler rack. Split and toast rolls. Place meat patty on each bottom half of roll, cover with sauce, add peaches, sprinkle with almonds and top with other half of roll.

Eight Burgers

Bluebeard

With blue cheese, mayonnaise, and chopped chives.

1 small bunch chives
1 pound ground beef
2 tablespoons dry white
* wine*
¼ pound crumbled blue
* cheese*

Butter
4 hamburger rolls
Mayonnaise
Salt
4 lettuce leaves

Mince chives, mix with beef, wine and cheese. Shape into four patties. Pan fry in butter.

Oven heat rolls, split and spread with mayonnaise. Place meat on bottom half of roll, sprinkle with salt, cover with lettuce leaf and top half of roll.

Four Burgers

Burgers Aglio-Olio

With olive oil, garlic, chopped parsley, orégano and grated Parmesan cheese.

2 cloves garlic	*½ teaspoon salt*
8-10 sprigs parsley	*½ teaspoon pepper*
¼ cup olive oil	*2 tablespoons ice water*
⅛ teaspoon orégano	*4 hamburger rolls*
1 pound ground beef	*2 tablespoons butter*
3-4 drops Angostura bit-	*3 tablespoons grated Par-*
ters	*mesan cheese*

Peel and mince garlic, chop parsley fine. Add to olive oil in small saucepan. Cook, stirring until garlic is limp. Stir in orégano.

Mix meat with Angostura bitters, salt, pepper and ice water. Shape into four patties. Broil.

Split rolls, spread with butter, sprinkle with grated cheese, toast. Dip meat patties in olive oil, garlic and parsley mixture, place on bottom half of roll, then spoon a little more of olive oil mixture over surface. Cover with top half of roll.

Four Burgers

Burger Robért

With onion rings sautéed in butter, Sauce Robért, chopped fresh mushrooms and crisp pickle slices.

1 Bermuda onion	*1 teaspoon salt*
2 tablespoons butter	*½ teaspoon pepper*
½ cup Sauce Robért (bot- tled)	*4 tablespoons sweet ver- mouth*
Juice of ½ lemon	*4-6 large fresh mushrooms*
2 pounds ground beef	*8 hamburger rolls*
1 teaspoon Beau Mondé seasoning	*12 small pickles, sliced*

Peel and slice onion, break into rings. Sauté in butter until limp but not browned, add Sauce Robért and lemon juice. Heat but do not allow to boil.

Mix meat with Beau Mondé seasoning, salt, pepper and vermouth. Shape into 8 patties. Broil.

Coarsely chop mushrooms. Split and toast rolls. Add broiled meat patty to each bottom half of roll, sprinkle with mushrooms. Cover with onion rings and sauce. Add pickles and cover with top half of roll.

Eight Burgers

Peanut Vendor

With chopped peanuts and minced onion in the meat; mustard, bananas and lettuce on top.

1 pound ground beef	*Butter*
½ teaspoon salt	*1 banana*
½ teaspoon pepper	*Mustard*
2 tablespoons ice water	*4 lettuce leaves*
½ cup ground peanuts	*4 hamburger rolls*

Mix together beef, salt, pepper, ice water and peanuts. Shape into four patties. Pan fry in butter.

Mash banana with mustard to taste. Split and toast rolls, spread with banana mixture. Place meat patty on each bottom half of roll, add lettuce and top half of roll.

Four Burgers

Monterey

With Mexican fried beans, onions and grated American cheese.

1 *Bermuda onion*	*Pinch of orégano*
¼ *pound mild American cheese*	2 *tablespoons tomato ketchup*
1 *pound ground beef*	4 *hamburger rolls*
½ *teaspoon salt*	1 *cup Mexican fried beans**
1 *teaspoon pepper*	
⅛ *teaspoon chili powder*	

Peel and chop onion. Grate cheese.

Mix beef with salt, pepper, chili powder, orégano and tomato ketchup. Shape into four patties. Broil.

Split and toast rolls. Spread with beans. Add meat patty to each roll bottom. Sprinkle with chopped onions and grated cheese. Cover with top half of roll.

Four Burgers

Triple Burger

With Roquefort cheese, purple onion slices, butter, pimiento stuffed green olives and parsley.

* See Chapter 5, page 66.

1 large purple onion	*8 hamburger rolls*
2 pounds ground beef	*Soft butter*
1 teaspoon salt	*¼ pound crumbled*
1 teaspoon Beau Mondé	*Roquefort cheese*
seasoning	*24 pimiento stuffed green*
4 tablespoons cream	*olives*

Peel and cut onion into thin slices.

Mix meat with salt, Beau Mondé seasoning, and cream. Shape into eight patties. Broil.

Split rolls, spread each half with soft butter, place onion slice on roll bottom, spread onion with butter, sprinkle both halves of roll with crumbled Roquefort cheese. Toast until cheese is melted. Place broiled meat patty on bottom half of roll, cover with top half. Spear olives with cocktail picks, stick in center of roll.

Eight Burgers

Burl Ives

With frankfurters, beer-barbecue sauce and dill pickle.

1 cup barbecue sauce	*1 teaspoon salt*
(bottled)	*½ cup beer*
4-6 dashes Tabasco sauce	*3 pounds ground beef*
1 clove garlic	*6 frankfurters*
1 tablespoon Worcester-	*12 hamburger rolls*
shire sauce	*24 thin slices of dill pickle*
1 tablespoon mustard	

To make sauce: Mix together first seven ingredients. Let stand at room temperature for one hour or longer.

Shape meat into twelve patties; cut frankfurters in

half, lengthwise; broil both on same rack, basting frequently with sauce. Split rolls and heat in oven. Dip cut sides of rolls into sauce, add meat patty to each roll bottom, cover with frankfurter, dill pickle slices and top half of roll.

Twelve Burgers

Double Devil Burger

With Cheddar cheese, fried onion rings, piccalilli and hot mustard.

2 pounds ground beef	*8 hamburger rolls*
¼ teaspoon celery salt	*¼ pound sharp Cheddar*
1 tablespoon grated onion	*cheese spread*
2 tablespoons horseradish	*Hot (Dijon type) mustard*
2 tablespoons ketchup	*1 small can French fried*
¼ teaspoon salt	*onions*
1 teaspoon pepper	*½ cup piccalilli*

Mix beef with celery salt, onion, horseradish, ketchup, salt and pepper. Shape meat into eight patties. Broil. Split rolls, spread with Cheddar cheese and toast until cheese is melted. Place meat patty on roll bottom, spread with mustard. Sprinkle with onion rings and piccalilli. Cover with top half of roll.

Eight Burgers

Cossack

With liverwurst slices, chopped mustard pickles and watercress.

½ *cup mustard pickles*
Small bunch watercress
1 *pound ground beef*
½ *teaspoon salt*
1 *teaspoon coarse ground*
  black pepper

2 *tablespoons dry Ver-*
  mouth
4 *hamburger rolls*
Soft butter
4 *slices liverwurst*

Coarsely chop pickles, chop watercress fine and combine.

Mix meat with salt, pepper, and Vermouth. Shape into four patties. Broil. Split and toast rolls, spread with soft butter. Place broiled meat patty on each roll bottom. Cover with liverwurst, pickles, watercress and top half of roll.

Four Burgers

Gandhi

With shredded green cabbage, sliced sautéed banana and chopped chutney.

⅙ *head of green cabbage*
  (approximate)
½ *cup chutney (bottled)*
1 *pound ground beef*
1 *teaspoon Accent*
2 *tablespoons ice water*

1 *tablespoon grated onion*
1 *banana*
2 *tablespoons butter*
4 *hamburger rolls*
Salt

Finely chop cabbage, place in mixing bowl. Finely chop any large pieces of chutney. Combine with cabbage.

Mix together ground beef, Accent, ice water and grated onion. Shape into four patties. Broil.

While meat cooks, slice banana; sauté slices in butter

over low flame until well heated but still firm. Split and toast rolls. Spoon some of the butter from the bananas on each roll bottom. Add meat patty, top with banana slices, cabbage-chutney mixture and top half of roll.

Four Burgers

Deliburger

With chopped onion, hard cooked egg slices, sour cream dressing, and watercress.

1 small Bermuda onion	*Salt*
1 hard cooked egg	*4 hamburger rolls*
1 pound ground beef	*Sour cream dressing**
2 tablespoons ice water	*Chopped watercress*

Chop onion fine and set aside. Cut hard cooked egg into thin slices and set aside.

Cover bottom of large cast iron skillet with salt; place over medium high heat. Mix meat with ice water, shape into four patties, add to pan. Cook three to four minutes on each side. Split rolls and heat in medium (375°) oven. Place a meat patty on a roll bottom. Spoon sour cream dressing on top, sprinkle with chopped onion. Add hard cooked egg slices and chopped watercress. Cover with top half of roll.

Four Burgers

Tijuana

With chili sauce, crushed Fritos, onion rings and chopped lettuce.

* *See Chapter 5, page 74.*

1 *small bag Frito corn chips*	2 *tablespoons ice water*
½ *small head lettuce*	½ *teaspoon salt*
1 *small Bermuda onion*	½ *cup chili sauce*
2 *pounds ground beef*	8 *hamburger rolls*
	Salt

Crumble Fritos and coarsely chop lettuce. Cut onion into thin slices, break into rings and set aside.

Mix meat with ice water and salt, shape into patties. Broil. While meat broils, heat chili sauce. Split and toast rolls. Add cooked meat patties to roll bottoms. Cover with onion rings, lettuce, chili sauce and top half of roll.

Eight Burgers

Gringo

With chili, Mexican fried beans, grated Monterey Jack cheese, lettuce and chopped onion.

1 *small onion*	2 *tablespoons dry vermouth*
¼ *small head lettuce*	
¼ *pound Monterey Jack cheese*	½ *teaspoon pepper*
¾ *cup chili sauce**	4 *hamburger rolls*
1 *pound ground beef*	1 *cup Mexican fried beans**
½ *teaspoon Tabasco sauce*	

Chop onion and lettuce fine. Grate cheese, set aside. Place chili sauce in heavy saucepan over very low flame.

Mix ground meat with Tabasco sauce, vermouth and pepper. Shape into four patties. Pan fry in butter.

* *See Chapter 5, page 77, or use bottled sauce for chili sauce; see page 66 for fried beans.*

Heat rolls in oven. Split, place one meat patty on each roll bottom. Spoon on chili and Mexican fried beans, sprinkle with onion, lettuce and cheese. Cover with top half of roll.

Four Burgers

Apple Danish

With fried apple rings, cinnamon, crisp bacon, horse-radish sauce.

1 large crisp apple	*1 pound ground beef*
1 tablespoon butter	*2 tablespoons ice water*
¼ teaspoon cinnamon	*Salt*
1 teaspoon sugar	*4 hamburger rolls*
4 slices bacon	*¼ cup horseradish sauce**

Slice and core apple. Sauté slices in butter until crisp-tender. Sprinkle with cinnamon and sugar, cover and set aside. Cook bacon in heavy skillet until crisp. Remove from pan. Pour off bacon grease. Mix meat with ice water, shape into four patties, pan fry in same skillet, sprinkle with salt. Split and toast rolls, place a meat patty on each bottom roll, add bacon and apple slices. Spoon on horseradish sauce. Cover with top half of roll.

Four Burgers

Babyburger

With peanut butter, crisp bacon, guava jelly and fresh crisp spinach leaves.

* See Chapter 5, page 74.

1 pound ground beef   *4 hamburger rolls*
2 tablespoons ice water   *Peanut butter*
Butter   *Guava jelly*
Salt   *4 raw spinach leaves*
4 slices bacon

Mix meat with ice water, shape into four patties. Pan fry in butter. When done, sprinkle with salt. Pan fry bacon.

Split and toast rolls. Spread roll bottoms with peanut butter and jelly. Add cooked meat patty, spinach leaf, and top half of roll.

Four Burgers

Bermuda

With sliced cucumber, Roquefort dressing, chopped chives and parsley.

Small bunch chives   *1 tablespoon molasses*
6 to 8 sprigs parsley   *1 tablespoon ice water*
1 large cucumber   *1 tablespoon prepared*
1 pound ground beef   *mustard*
1 teaspoon Accent   *Butter*
¾ teaspoon salt   *4 hamburger rolls*
½ teaspoon coarse ground   *½ cup Roquefort cheese*
*   black pepper*   *dressing*

Chop chives and parsley fine. Cut cucumber into paper-thin slices. Mix together beef, Ac'cent, salt, pepper, molasses, ice water and mustard. Shape into four patties. Pan fry.

Split and toast rolls. Place cooked meat patty on each roll bottom, add cucumber slices and Roquefort dressing, sprinkle with chopped chives and parsley. Cover with top half of roll.

Four Burgers

Manhattan

With anchovies, sour cream, and onion rings marinated in dressing.

1 Bermuda onion	*2 tablespoons ice water*
*¼ cup French dressing**	*1 teaspoon salt*
1 pound ground beef	*4 hamburger rolls*
¼ teaspoon Beau Mondé	*8 anchovy fillets*
seasoning	*¼ cup sour cream*

Slice onion, marinate at room temperature in French dressing one hour or longer.

Mix beef with Beau Mondé seasoning, ice water and salt. Shape into four patties. Pan fry.

Split and toast rolls. Place one cooked meat patty on bottom half of each roll. Top with anchovy fillets, drained onion slices, sour cream and top half of roll.

Four Burgers

Florida Burger

With parsley butter and orange slices marinated in French dressing.

---

* *See Chapter 5, page 75, or use bottled dressing.*

8-10 sprigs parsley	*1 teaspoon salt*
4 tablespoons butter	*1 teaspoon pepper*
2 large seedless oranges	*4 tablespoons cream*
½ cup French dressing*	*8 hamburger rolls*
2 pounds ground beef	

Chop parsley fine, add to butter and cream until smooth. Peel and slice oranges, place in flat bottomed non-metal bowl. Cover with French dressing. Allow to stand at room temperature one hour or longer.

Mix meat with salt, pepper and cream. Shape into eight patties and broil.

Split and toast rolls, spread with parsley butter. Add meat patty to roll bottom, cover with well drained orange slices and top half of roll.

Eight Burgers

España

With tomato sauce and chopped celery, scallions, and green pepper cooked in olive oil.

1 cup tomato sauce**	*1 teaspoon coarse ground*
3 stalks celery	*black pepper*
6 scallions	*⅓ cup dry red wine*
1 small green pepper	*12 hamburger rolls*
3 tablespoons olive oil	*Salt*
3 pounds ground beef	

Place tomato sauce in top of double boiler over simmering water.

Chop celery, scallions and green pepper medium fine. Sauté in olive oil until limp.

---

* *See Chapter 5, page 75.*
** *See Chapter 5, page 78, or use canned sauce.*

Mix meat with wine and pepper. Shape into twelve patties. Broil.

Split and toast rolls. Use long forks to dip each broiled meat patty in sauce, then place on bottom half of roll. Sprinkle with salt. Spoon celery-scallion-green pepper mixture plus a little additional sauce over meat. Cover with top half of roll.

Twelve Burgers

Burger Barbecue

With barbecue sauce and that great outdoors flavor.

2 pounds ground beef   *Barbecue sauce**
4 tablespoons ice water   *8 hamburger rolls*

Blend meat with ice water, shape into eight patties. Heat sauce in long-handled sauce pan on grill. Grill patties over coals, basting frequently with warm barbecue sauce.

To prevent meat from sticking to grill: brush each patty on both sides with oil just before placing on grill.

Serve on heated rolls with more sauce spooned over meat. To heat rolls: Put in large coffee can, cover, and place on grill. Turn can frequently so that all sides are heated evenly.

Tips: Forget about usual cooking timetables. They rarely apply out of doors. The heat of the coals, the unpredictable wind, even the size and shape of the grill are variables that effect timing. If you can't tell when the meat is done by looking at it, cut a tiny

---

* *Try these sauces: Chili-Horseradish-Sauce-on-the-Meat (page 75), Easy Barbecue Sauce (page 76), Red Wine Barbecue Sauce (page 76), Texas Barbecue Sauce (page 76) or Dry Sauce (page 77).*

slit in the thickest part of the patty and judge by the color of the meat in the center.

Eight Burgers

If your grill is adjustable, place it about three inches from glowing coals. For rare burgers grill seven to ten minutes on each side. The difference depends on the intensity of heat.

Start your fire early. To reach the "glowing coal" stage necessary for cooking hamburgers takes at least two hours or more. You are ready to start only when your fuel—regular charcoal, charcoal bricketts or seasoned wood—is down to radiant embers topped by gray ash.

Shape meat patties ahead if desired. (Seasoning may be added before cooking. However, it is usually not needed as barbecue sauce is highly seasoned and penetrates into meat as it cooks.)

Refrigerate raw meat patties, well covered, for as long as possible before bringing outdoors. If your barbecue is to be some distance away, freeze meat well wrapped in foil with a double thickness of paper between each. Pack wrapped package in picnic hamper. Unwrap at site. They will thaw in two to three hours or may be grilled frozen.

Super Better Burgers with "Butter Plus"

With garlic Dill Butter, Parsley Butter, Roquefort Butter, Fresh Tomato Butter, Peanut Butter, Bacon Butter, Butter Sauce Robért, Horseradish Butter, Garlic Butter, Curried Chutney Butter, Anchovy Butter, Parmesan Butter or Herb Butter.*

* See Chapter 5, page 85.

1 *pound ground round*   2 *tablespoons crushed ice*
  steak, mixed with 2   4 *hamburger rolls*
  ounces ground beef suet   *Flavored butter*
1 *teaspoon salt*   *Pickles*
½ *teaspoon freshly ground*   *Tomato wedges*
  black pepper   *Lettuce leaves*

Mix meat with salt, pepper and crushed ice. Broil, pan-fry or fry in salt to desired degree of rareness.

Split and toast rolls. Spread both halves with flavored butter. Put together with meat patty. Garnish plate with tomato wedges and pickles on crisp lettuce leaves.

"Butter plus" or "compounded butter," call it what you will—is just another way of adding lots of flavor with little effort. French chefs know its value and have used it for years. There is nothing new about it except the selection of ingredients but for hamburgers its ideal.

Just remember to start with room temperature, soft but never melted butter. Use a wooden spoon to cream butter and blend in other ingredients, then beat with wire wisk or fork to obtain a light fluffy mixture.

Make it ahead, if you like, even days before. Store, well sealed with foil or plastic wrap, in refrigerator or freezer. Be sure to remove it from the cold and let stand at room temperature until soft enough to spread easily before using.

Four Burgers

3

Fork Burgers

Au Poivre

With crushed peppercorns, shallots, cognac and red wine.

3-4 *shallots*
4-5 *tablespoons pepper-corns*
1½ *pounds chopped sir-loin*
2 *tablespoons butter*
4 *Hamburger rolls*

2 *tablespoons cognac*
1 *cup dry red wine*
1 *tablespoon Sauce Diable (bottled)*
Salt
Chopped parsley for gar-nish (optional)

Peel and chop shallots. Crush peppercorns with mortar and pestle, or crush them on a flat surface with the bottom of a heavy skillet. The peppercorns must not be too fine. Shape meat into eight patties. Dip patties, one at a time, into crushed peppercorns, lightly pressing pepper into surface of meat. Heat one tablespoon of the butter in a heavy skillet, pan fry meat to desired degree of rareness.

Oven heat rolls, split. Place meat patty on each half of roll. To keep warm, cover lightly with aluminum foil while making sauce.

Add shallots to skillet, stir and quickly add cognac and wine. Bring to a boil, stir in remaining butter and Sauce Diable. Cook, stirring only until butter melts. Pour over meat patties. Sprinkle with salt and chopped parsley if desired.

Eight Burgers

Imperial

With liver paté, Bordeaux wine sauce, mushroom and sautéed-in-butter toast.

4 slices white bread	*3 tablespoons butter*
1 pound ground beef	*½ teaspoon salt*
1 teaspoon coarse ground black pepper	*4 slices liver paté*
¾ cup Bordeaux (dry red) wine	*4 large fresh mushroom caps*

Mix meat with pepper, shape into four patties, place in non-metal bowl. Cover with wine. Let stand at room temperature one hour or longer.

Trim crust from bread. Flatten each slice slightly with rolling pin. Cut into rounds a little larger than hamburger rolls.

Sauté bread slices in one tablespoon of the butter in large heavy skillet. Remove to ovenproof platter. Place in 200° F. oven. Add second tablespoon butter to skillet. Pan fry meat patties three minutes on each side. Place on bread slices. Cover each with slice of liver paté. Cover platter with aluminum foil, return to oven. Sauté mushroom caps in same pan in third tablespoon of butter.

Place on top of liver paté and meat. Pour remaining wine in which meat was marinated into skillet. Cook over high heat until reduced to half. Pour over hamburgers. Serve from platter.

Four Burgers

Duchess

On toasted buttered rye bread, with Duchess potatoes and sliced tomato.

1 large ripe tomato	*2 tablespoons heavy*
1 pound ground beef	*cream*
¼ teaspoon orégano	*Butter*
½ teaspoon black pepper	*4 slices rye bread*
½ teaspoon salt	*Duchess potatoes**

Cut tomato into four thick slices, discarding end pieces.

Mix meat with orégano, pepper, salt and cream. Shape into four patties. Pan fry in butter.

Toast bread on one side only. Butter untoasted side, place meat patty in center. Top with tomato slice. Surround with Duchess potatoes, covering edges of bread completely.

Place butter slivers on tomato slice and potatoes. Place under broiler and broil until potatoes are lightly browned.

Four Burgers

* See Chapter 5, page 66.

Burgers All-In-One

With absolutely standard ingredients but cooked in a different way.

4 hamburger rolls	*2 tablespoons chili sauce*
Butter	*(bottled)*
1 pound ground beef	*1 tablespoon Worcester-*
1 teaspoon coarse ground	*shire sauce*
black pepper	*2-4 drops Tabasco sauce*
1 teaspoon salt	*8 slices bacon*
½ teaspoon Beau Mondé	
seasoning	

Split rolls, butter both halves.

Mix meat with pepper, salt, Beau Mondé seasoning, chili sauce, Worcestershire sauce and Tabasco sauce. Blend well. Cover each half of the rolls completely with meat mixture. Cut bacon slices in half. Place crosswise over meat. Place under broiler. Broil until bacon is crisp and meat is done to taste.

Four Burgers

Hotel Plaza Athenée

On toasted French bread, topped with soft poached egg with freshly ground black pepper and coarse salt and sour pickle and lettuce leaf garnish.

4 slices French bread	*4 eggs*
1 pound ground beef	*Sour pickle slices*
2 tablespoons dry red	*Lettuce leaves*
wine	*Coarse salt*
½ teaspoon salt	*Black pepper*
2 tablespoons butter	

Wrap French bread slices loosely in foil, seal edges. Place in 300° F. oven to heat.

Mix meat with wine and salt, shape into four large flat patties. Heat a skillet, add meat patty, brown on both sides over very high heat. Add remaining butter, continue cooking only until butter has melted. Cover skillet, remove from heat, keep warm on back of stove. Poach eggs.

Place meat patties on warm toast. Cover with just poached eggs. Garnish plate with sour pickle slices and lettuce leaves. Pass course salt and pepper mill at the table.

Four Burgers

Tartare Burger

With capers, chopped onion and twice ground raw meat.

2 hamburger rolls
Butter
Garlic salt
1 pound sirloin
1 small onion
1 teaspoon salt
¾ teaspoon freshly ground black pepper

1 teaspoon Worcestershire sauce
1 egg yolk
3 tablespoons capers
Garnish of chopped parsley, chopped oinion, capers.

Peel and chop onion fine.

Split and lightly butter rolls, sprinkle lightly with garlic salt. Place in 200° F. oven, bake until crisp and dry as melba toast.

Trim all fat from meat. Grind twice just before serving, or have your butcher do it, preferably no more than one hour before serving. Mix meat with remaining ingredients. Spoon equally over roll halves. Surround with garnish of chopped onion, capers and chopped parsley.

Four Burgers

Toasted Hero Mexicano

With shredded lettuce, avocado slices, tomato and Queso enchilado.

¼ head iceburg lettuce	*1½ pounds ground beef*
1 avocado	*1 teaspoon salt*
1 small tomato	*3 tablespoons Mexican*
4 slices of Queso enchil-	*beer*
ado (sharp Mexican	*4 hero sandwich buns*
cheese)	*"Garlicy" mayonnaise**

Coarsely chop lettuce. Peel and slice avocado. Cut tomato in half, press out seeds and juice, cut into strips.

Mix meat with salt and beer. Shape into eight patties. Broil.

Split buns. Tear out soft centers. Spread with "Garlicy" mayonnaise. Fill with chopped lettuce, avocado slices and tomato strips. Place meat patties on top. Cover with cheese. Place under broiler and broil until cheese melts.

Eight Burgers

Henry VIII

On toasted French rolls with Burgundy Sauce, served with green onions and raw cauliflower buds.

* See Chapter 5, page 74.

1 *clove garlic*
1 *teaspoon salt*
1 *cup Burgundy (dry red) wine*
Juice of 1 lemon
½ *cup olive oil*
1 *teaspoon black pepper*
½ *teaspoon orégano*

1 *tablespoon sugar*
2 *pounds ground beef*
1 *teaspoon coarse ground black pepper*
1 *teaspoon salt*
2 *tablespoons crushed ice*
4 *large French rolls*

Crush garlic clove with salt, add wine, lemon juice, oil, pepper, orégano and sugar.

Mix meat with pepper, salt and crushed ice. Broil. Heat wine mixture, use to baste meat frequently while broiling. Oven heat rolls, split, place one meat patty on each roll half. Spoon remaining wine mixture over surface. Garnish plate with green onions and raw cauliflower buds.

Eight Burgers

Sicilian Joe

With a sauce of anchovies, black olives, capers, and parsley, served in scooped out Italian rolls.

6-8 *anchovy fillets*
1 *tablespoon capers*
6-8 *black olives*
4-6 *parsley sprigs*
1 *clove garlic*
1 *tablespoon olive oil*

1 *cup tomato sauce**
1½ *pounds ground beef*
2 *tablespoons butter*
4 *large crusty Italian rolls*
4 *tablespoons grated Parmesan cheese*

Drain, cut up and crush anchovies; drain capers; pit and chop black olives; chop parsley; mince garlic. Heat

oil with garlic in saucepan, add tomato sauce, ancho-

* *See Chapter 5, page 78, or use canned sauce.*

vies, capers, olives and parsley. Cook, stirring three to four minutes.

Cook meat in butter in heavy skillet, stirring with fork until meat has broken up and lost its red color. Combine with sauce mixture, cook, stirring one to two minutes longer.

Scoop out soft centers from rolls, fill with meat mixture. Sprinkle with cheese. Place under broiler and broil until cheese is melted.

Eight Burgers

Southwestern

With kidney beans, chopped onion, chili sauce and grated American cheese.

1 *can red kidney beans*	1 *clove garlic, minced*
1 *cup tomato sauce**	1 *large Bermuda onion*
½ *teaspoon chili powder*	½ *pound American cheese*
2-3 *drops Tabasco sauce*	2 *pounds ground beef*
½ *teaspoon cayenne*	1 *teaspoon salt*
pepper	1 *teaspoon pepper*
½ *teaspoon coarse ground*	4 *tablespoons crushed ice*
black pepper	4 *hamburger rolls*

Combine first seven ingredients in heavy saucepan. Simmer gently over low heat for thirty minutes.

Peel and chop onion. Grate cheese.

Mix meat with salt, pepper and ice. Shape into four patties. Broil.

Split and toast rolls. Place a broiled meat patty on each roll half. Spoon bean sauce on top. Sprinkle with chopped onion and grated cheese.

Eight Burgers

* *See Chapter 5, page 78, or use canned sauce.*

Left Bank

With sautéed parsley, tomato slices and garlic butter.

1 *large ripe tomato*	1 *tablespoon Dijon mus-*
8-10 *sprigs parsley*	*tard*
1 *clove garlic*	2 *tablespoons crushed ice*
1 *pound ground beef*	2 *tablespoons butter*
½ *teaspoon salt*	4 *large French rolls*
1 *teaspoon pepper*	

Cut tomato into four slices, discarding end pieces. Chop parsley, mince garlic.

Mix meat with salt, pepper, mustard and ice water. Shape into four patties. Broil.

Heat butter with garlic in saucepan, stir in parsley. Split rolls and heat in the oven. Place broiled meat patties on bottom halves of rolls, tomato slices on top halves. Pour garlic-parsley butter over both. Serve as open face hamburgers.

Four Burgers

Cook at the Table Party Skillet Burgers

2 *hamburger rolls*	*Coarse ground black pep-*
1 *pound ground sirloin*	*per*
Salt	*Butter*
	*Choice of sauces**

---

* *Serve with any of the following sauces: Dublin Butter Sauce (page 79), Mustard Butter Sauce (page 79), Devil Sauce (page 80), Parsley Butter Sauce (page 80), Sherry Mushroom Sauce (page 80), Cheese and Beer sauce (page 81), Tomato Cheese Sauce (page 81), Olive Sauce (page 80), Sauce à la Creme (page 82) or Anchovy Brown Sauce (page 82).*

Split rolls. Wrap loosely in aluminum foil, sealing edges of foil. Place in 350° F. oven for ten minutes. To keep warm, bring to table wrapped. Do not unwrap until meat is cooked.

Shape meat into four patties, sprinkle liberally with salt and pepper, gently press seasoning into surface of meat. Pan fry in butter in electric skillet or in a chafing dish to desired degree of rareness. Place on warm roll halves, cover lightly with aluminum foil while making sauce.

Wipe out skillet with paper toweling, then prepare sauce in it; pour sauce over meat patties and serve.

Four Burgers

4

Filled Burgers

MASTER RECIPE FOR FILLED BURGERS

2 pounds ground beef
1½ teaspoons salt
3 tablespoons heavy
  cream

Fillings (see below)
8 hamburger rolls

Mix meat with salt and cream. Shape into sixteen patties half as thick as usual. Put two together with filling between, making eight burgers. Press edges together. Broil or pan fry as usual.

Split rolls and heat in the oven. Place a patty on roll bottom and cover with top half of roll.

Eight Burgers

MUSHROOM FILLING

4-5 large fresh mushrooms
1 teaspoon butter
1-2 tablespoons heavy
  cream

⅛ teaspoon salt
⅛ teaspoon pepper

Chop mushrooms fine, sauté in butter two to three minutes. Stir in sufficient cream to bind. Season with salt and pepper.

CREOLE FILLING

2 *tablespoons onion*
1 *tablespoon minced celery*
1 *tablespoon minced green pepper*
1 *tablespoon butter*

2 *tablespoons tomato ketchup*
1 *tablespoon tomato paste*
2-3 *dashes of Tabasco sauce*
¼ *teaspoon salt*

Sauté onion, celery and green pepper in butter until limp but not browned. Stir in remaining ingredients. Cool before filling burgers.

ROQUEFORT FILLING

3 *tablespoons Roquefort cheese*

2 *tablespoons heavy cream*

Crumble cheese, mix with cream until blended but do not cream.

TOMATO OLIVE FILLING

1 *tomato*
6-8 *stuffed green olives*
½ *teaspoon olive oil*

⅛ *teaspoon pepper*
salt

Coarsely chop tomato. Cook over medium heat until reduced to thick pulp. (Chop with tip of spatula while cooking. Stir often). Chop olives and add with olive oil, salt and pepper. Cool before filling burgers.

BACON FILLING

3-4 *slices crisp-cooked*   1 *tablespoon mustard*
     bacon   1 *tablespoon mayonnaise*
10-12 *sweet mixed pickles*

Crumble bacon, chop pickles. Mix with remaining ingredients.

SWISS CHEESE AND DILL PICKLE FILLING

2-3 *slices Swiss cheese*   1-2 *tablespoons Sauce*
1 *medium dill pickle*   *Diablé (bottled)*
1 *small onion*

Cut cheese into thin slivers, chop pickle and onion, mix together. Bind together with Sauce Diablé.

ALMOND FILLING

2 *tablespoons grated*   2-3 *drops Tabasco sauce*
     almonds   1 *tablespoon heavy*
2-3 *tablespoons cream*   *cream*
     cheese

Combine ingredients. Blend, then cream until light and smooth.

ONION CHEESE FILLING

2 *tablespoons crumbled*   1 *tablespoon mayonnaise*
     sharp cheese   2-3 *drops Tabasco sauce*
2 *tablespoons chopped*
     onion

Combine ingredients, blend well.

WALNUT FILLING

2 tablespoons chopped   *1 tablespoon prepared*
walnuts   *horseradish*
                                           2 tablespoons mayonnaise

Combine ingredients, blend well.

FETA CHEESE FILLING

3 tablespoons crumbled   *1 tablespoon chopped*
Feta cheese   *chives*
6-8 Greek black olives   *2 tablespoons heavy*
                                            cream

Combine ingredients, mix well but do not cream.

BURGERS THAT WAIT

Season ground beef to taste, shape as usual into patties. Pan fry in butter. Split hamburger rolls. Spread with softened butter. Put together with meat patty and slice of mild cheese. Secure with cocktail picks. Wrap prepared burgers loosely in foil. Seal edges of foil. Place in 300° F. oven.

They will be ready to serve in about fifteen minutes but can "wait" for thirty to forty-five minutes.

Instead of cheese slice, spread rolls with chive cream cheese, sprinkle with chopped onion, add meat patty. Wrap and bake.

Or: substitute crusty hero buns for hamburger rolls. Remove soft center. Fill with grated swiss cheese before adding meat.

Or: spread rolls before adding meat with Mexican fried beans, add a slice of avocado and a sprinkling of chopped chives.

Or: substitute one long loaf of french bread for rolls. Scoop out soft center. Spread with olive oil, sprinkle with lemon juice and line bottom half with well drained anchovies. Add four to six cooked meat patties, cover with top half of loaf and secure with cocktail picks. Wrap and bake. Slice at the table.

Burgers "Look Under"—1

With avocado slices, pimento and Cheddar cheese.

1½ *pounds ground top* *round*	1 *avocado*
1 *teaspoon pepper*	1 *small can pimento*
1 *teaspoon salt*	4 *hamburger rolls*
2 *tablespoons cream*	8 *slices Cheddar cheese*

Mix meat, salt, pepper, and cream, shape into eight patties. Broil.

Peel and slice avocado, drain pimentos. Split rolls and place a cooked meat patty on each half. Cover with avocado slices and pieces of pimento. Top each with cheese slice. Place under broiler. Broil until cheese is melted.

Eight Burgers

Burgers "Look Under"—2

With liverwurst, corn relish, chili sauce and mild American cheese.

1½ pounds ground beef
1 teaspoon salt
1 green pepper
2 tablespoons cold beer
4 hamburger rolls
Butter

4 tablespoons corn relish
4 tablespoons chili sauce
8 slices liverwurst
8 slices mild American cheese

Mix meat, salt, pepper and beer. Shape into eight patties. Broil.

Split and toast rolls, spread each half lightly with butter, top each with cooked meat patty, corn relish, chili sauce, slice of liverwurst and cheese slice. Place under broiler and broil until cheese is melted.

Eight Burgers

Burgers "Look Under"—3

With parsley-tomato slice sautéed in "garlicy" olive oil and Mozzarella chese.

1 large ripe tomato
1 clove garlic
3-4 sprigs parsley
1 pound ground beef
½ teaspoon freshly
    ground black pepper
½ teaspoon salt

¼ teaspoon thyme
2 tablespoons ketchup
2 tablespoons olive oil
2 hamburger rolls
Butter
4 slices Mozzarella cheese

Cut tomato into four thick slices, discarding end pieces. Peel and mince garlic, chop parsley fine.

Mix meat with pepper, salt, thyme and ketchup. Shape into four patties. Broil.

While meat broils, heat olive oil with garlic, add tomato slices. Cook over medium heat for two minutes, turn and sprinkle with parsley. Cover pan and cook two minutes longer. Split rolls and spread with butter. Add a meat patty to each butter roll half; top with parsley-tomato slice. Cover with cheese slice. Place under broiler. Broil until cheese is melted.

Burgers "Look Under"—4

With chopped onion, "drunken raisins," sweet mixed pickles, ketchup and Gruyère cheese.

½ *cup raisins*	3 *tablespoons ketchup*
2 *tablespoons blended*	½ *teaspoon pepper*
whiskey	½ *teaspoon salt*
1 *small Bermuda onion*	¼ *teaspoon ground*
¼ *cup sweet mixed*	*ginger*
pickles	8 *slices light rye bread*
1 *tablespoon butter*	*Butter*
1½ *pounds ground beef*	8 *slices Gruyére cheese*

Combine raisins and whiskey, let stand one hour or longer. Peel and chop onion. Chop pickles fine. Heat butter in large skillet and add onions. Cook until limp but not browned. Add meat. Cook, stirring with fork, until no longer pink. Drain raisins, add to meat with pickle, ketchup, pepper, salt and ginger. Blend well.

Toast bread on one side only. Spread untoasted sides with butter, cover with meat mixture and top with cheese slices. Place under broiler. Broil until cheese is melted.

Eight Burgers

Burgers "Look Under"—6

With chopped peanuts and grated Monterey Jack cheese.

1½ pounds ground beef   *4 hamburger rolls*
1 tablespoon butter   *¾ cup chopped peanuts*
¾ teaspoon salt   *1 cup grated Monterey*
1 teaspoon pepper   *Jack cheese*
⅛ teaspoon garlic salt

Cook beef with butter in heavy skillet over medium heat, stir with fork until broken up and no longer pink. Season with salt, pepper and garlic salt. Split rolls, tear out soft center. Spoon meat over entire surface. Mix together peanuts and cheese, sprinkle liberally over meat. Place under broiler. Broil until cheese is melted.

Eight Burgers

5

"Go Withs"

What goes with a hamburger? Pickles do. Sweet and sour pickles, dill pickles, pickled beans and pickled beets, to name a few.

So does salad: Mixed green, cole slaw, guacamole, potato, tomato, and cucumber and many, many others, of course.

Then potato chips go with hamburgers, as every one knows, but so do corn chips, potato sticks, and fried chips of green banana or yams.

Some other things we can think of are: radishes, green onions, carrot sticks, raw turnip slices, celery, tomatoes, raw spinach and lettuce—romaine, iceberg and bib.

For drinks: Tops on our list are milk, cokes, beer and red wine. Though we really have nothing against chilled rosé, lemonade, gin and tonic or even martinis on the rocks.

What doesn't go with hamburgers? We really don't know but here are a few "go withs" we do find exceptionally good.

Absolutely Perfect French Fried Potatoes

Peel large uniform Idaho or Maine potatoes. Cut into pieces about two inches long, half inch thick. Dry them well on paper towel. Fill large pot with cooking oil to three-quarters of the rim. Heat to 375° F. on deep fat thermometer. Add potatoes, a few at a time. Do not crowd pan. Cook eight to ten minutes or until potatoes are soft but just starting to turn brown. Remove from fat with slotted spoon, drain well on paper toweling. Heat fat to 400° F., return potatoes to pan, again only a few at a time, cook for one to two minutes or until they are crisp and golden brown. Drain, sprinkle with salt and serve.

Sweet Potato Chips

Sweet Potatoes   *Salt*
Oil

Peel potatoes, cut crosswise into very thin slices. Soak in salted ice water fifteen to thirty minutes. Drain, pat dry. Fry in deep hot oil (400° F.) until crisp and lightly browned. Drain on paper toweling. Sprinkle with salt. Serve warm.

Note: As with all such food, the amount per serving of Sweet Potato Chips or Green Banana Chips depends on appetite. We find half banana—one-third sweet potato per person a good way to begin.

Banana Chips

Green bananas   *Salt*
Cooking oil

Peel bananas, slice thin (diagonally). Soak in cold salted water for fifteen minutes. Drain, pat dry. Fry in deep oil (at 400° F.) until golden brown and crisp. Sprinkle lightly with salt. Serve warm.

Duchess Potatoes

1 tablespoon butter   *1 egg yolk (slightly*
3 tablespoons heavy   *beaten)*
cream   *Salt*
1 cup (left over or freshly
cooked) mashed pota-
toes

Melt butter in saucepan, stir in cream. Heat thoroughly but do not allow to boil. Add to mashed potatoes. Blend well, add egg yolk and salt to taste, beat with fork until light and smooth.

Frijoles Refritos Pronto

(Quick Mexican Fried Beans)

2 (#2) cans red kidney   *2 tablespoons minced*
beans   *onion*
3-4 tablespoons fat*   *Salt to taste*

Drain beans but reserve liquid. Heat one tablespoon fat with the onion. Add about one third of the beans.

* *Mexican cooks use lard. You may substitute bacon fat or butter, if preferred.*

Mash and stir with fork until smooth and dry. Blend in some of the bean liquid. Continue adding fat, beans and liquid in that order until all ingredients have been used. Mixture should resemble rather dry mashed potatoes. Add additional fat or liquid if needed. Season to taste with salt. Serve hot with hamburgers or use as spread on toasted hamburger rolls.

Serves Eight

Ranch Beans

1 *pound pinto beans*
½ *pound salt pork,*
  cubed
1 *onion, peeled and diced*
1 *bay leaf*
3-4 *peppercorns*

1 *tablespoon brown sugar*
½ *cup chili sauce*
¼-½ *teaspoon chili*
  powder
Salt

Soak beans overnight in water to cover. Drain, place in large saucepan, cover with fresh water. Add salt pork, onion, bay leaf and peppercorns. Simmer gently over low heat until tender (about one hour and a half to two hours). Stir occasionally. Keep pan partially covered, add additional water if needed, but only a little at a time. There should be only a small amount of liquid when beans are done. Stir in sugar, chili sauce and chili powder. Cook ten minutes longer. Season with salt to taste.

Eight to Ten Servings

Easy Baked Beans

2 (#2) cans pork and   1 onion
  beans   3 tablespoons   blackstrap
2 slices thick-sliced, un-   molasses
  cooked bacon   ⅓ cup ketchup

Dice bacon, chop onion.
Combine ingredients in baking dish. Mix well. Bake,
covered, at 350° F. for thirty to forty minutes.

Serves Eight

Welsh Rabbit

2 tablespoons butter   2 cups shredded sharp
1 teaspoon salt   Cheddar cheese
1 teaspoon coarse ground   1—1½ cups beer or ale
  black pepper

Melt butter in top of double boiler or in chafing dish.
Add remaining ingredients, using one cup of beer or
ale. Stir until cheese is melted.

Keep warm over very low heat. Add more beer if
rabbit becomes too thick.

Rabbit may be made ahead and reheated. Cover and
refrigerate. Reheat with a little additional beer.

Banana and Bacon "Go With"

1 tablespoon sugar   2 bananas
1 tablespoon cinnamon   4 strips bacon cut in half

Mix together sugar and cinnamon. Peel bananas and
cut each banana in four slices (crosswise), roll in

sugar-cinnamon mixture. Wrap each piece in half of bacon strip. Broil, turning often, until bacon is crisp. Serve hot.

Makes Eight

Cucumbers in Horseradish Cream

2-3 *sprigs fresh parsley*
3-4 *large cucumbers*
½ *cup sour cream*
¼ *cup prepared*
horseradish

Chop parsley fine. Partially peel and cut cucumbers into paper thin slices. Mix together sour cream, horseradish and chopped parsley. Combine with cucumbers. Chill thoroughly before serving.

Serves Four to Six

Red Onions in Vinegar

2 *large red onions*
2-3 *sprigs parsley*
2-3 *sprigs mint leaves*
½ *teaspoon marjoram*
3 *tablespoons tarragon*
vinegar
4 *tablespoons olive oil*

Peel and cut onions into paper thin slices, break into rings. Place in a flat bottom non-metal bowl. Sprinkle with parsley and mint leaves. Mix vinegar with oil, blend and pour over onions. Cover and refrigerate three to four hours before serving. Drain, serve "on" or with hamburgers.

Six to Eight Servings

Cabbage Relish

2 large raw beets
½ head green cabbage
¼ head red cabbage
1 small Bermuda onion
½ cup prepared
   horseradish

2 tablespoons sugar
¼ cup cider vinegar
1 teaspoon salt
1 cup mayonnaise

Peel and chop beets. Chop cabbage fine. There should be enough green cabbage to make two cups and enough red to make one cup. Peel and slice onion, break into rings. Combine and add remaining ingredients. Toss well. Cover and let mellow in refrigerator three to four hours before serving. It is even better if made twelve to twenty-four hours ahead of time.

Guacamole

4 avocados
2 tablespoons salad oil
2 tablespoons lime or
   lemon juice
2 tablespoons chili sauce

1 finely minced onion
Salt
Pepper
1 small tomato

Peel and mash avocados, add remaining ingredients, except tomato. Whip with wire wisk or fork until light and fluffy. Plunge tomato into boiling water a half minute, rinse under cold water, rub off skin. Cut in half, press out seeds and juice, cut into thin strips. Fold into avocado mixture. Serve as salad on crisp lettuce leaves, as spread on hamburger rolls, or as a "go with" dip for potato or corn chips.

Note: Guacamole is best if not made ahead. However, if you must do so, place in non-metal salad bowl, add one or two avocado pits to mixture (this will keep it from turning color). Cover and leave in a cool place until ready to serve. It will taste better if not refrigerated.

Serves Eight as Salad

Guacamole for Spread

2 avocados	*Salt*
1 tablespoon salad oil	*Pepper*
1 tablespoon lemon juice	

Peel and mash avocados. Blend with oil and lemon juice. Season to taste with salt and pepper.

Potato Salad

4 cups diced boiled potatoes	*½ cup minced green pepper*
2 hard cooked eggs, diced	*Juice of ½ lemon*
4 tablespoons minced green onions	*2-3 dashes Tabasco sauce*
½ cup minced mixed sweet pickles	*1 teaspoon coarse ground black pepper*
2 cups minced celery	*1 teaspoon salt*
	1 cup mayonnaise

Place potatoes in large salad bowl with eggs, green onions, pickles, celery and green pepper. Combine lemon juice, Tabasco sauce, pepper, salt and mayonnaise, blend and pour over potato mixture. Mix together lightly. Correct seasoning with additional salt, if desired.

Caraway Seed Cole Slaw

1 *large cabbage*	1 *cup cream*
3 *egg yolks*	2-3 *tablespoons caraway*
½ *cup sugar*	*seeds*
1 *teaspoon salt*	¼ *cup mayonnaise*
2 *tablespoons butter*	1 *tablespoon prepared*
1 *cup white wine vinegar*	*mustard*

Chop cabbage fine, there should be enough to make six cups. Rinse cabbage in cold running water, drain well; cover and refrigerate until well chilled.

Mix egg yolks with sugar and salt. Combine with butter, vinegar and cream. Cook until thick in top half double boiler over simmering water. Stir often. Remove from heat. Chill in refrigerator.

Pour chilled dressing over well chilled cabbage, add caraway seeds and mayonnaise mixed with mustard. Toss until well blended.

Eight to Twelve Servings

Southern Pineapple Cole Slaw

1 *small head cabbage*	*Juice of ½ lemon*
1 *(#2) can crushed*	1 *teaspoon salt*
pineapple	1 *cup mayonnaise*

Chop cabbage fine, there should be enough to make three to four cups. Drain pineapple, mix with cabbage; add lemon juice, salt and mayonnaise. Toss until well blended. Refrigerate, covered, until well chilled. (Best if made twelve to twenty-four hours before serving.)

Eight Servings

Red Bean and Onion Salad

2 (#2) cans red kidney beans
¾ cup salad oil
½ cup wine vinegar
1 clove garlic
1 large Bermuda onion
½ teaspoon salt
½ teaspoon coarse ground black pepper
1 teaspoon sugar

Drain liquid from beans. Peel onion, slice and break into rings. Mix drained beans and onions with remaining ingredients. Cover, store in refrigerator twenty-four hours or longer. (Remove garlic clove after twelve hours.) Drain just before serving as salad on crisp lettuce leaves, or as a relish for hamburgers.

Eight Servings as Salad

Texas Tomato and Cucumber Salad

4-6 ripe tomatoes
2 large cucumbers
½ teaspoon salt
2 tablespoons minced parsley
1 tablespoon dried dill
1 tablespoon sugar
1 tablespoon minced onion
½ cup salad oil
¼ cup tarragon vinegar
1 head iceberg lettuce

Cut tomatoes into thin wedges. Peel and dice cucumber. Place in non-metal flat bottomed dish. Sprinkle with salt, parsley, dill, sugar and onion. Mix together oil and vinegar, pour over salad. Refrigerate, covered, for two hours or longer. Tear lettuce into bite-size pieces. Place in salad bowl. Add tomato-cucumber mixture. Toss well. Correct seasoning with additional salt if needed.

Serves Six to Eight

Sour Cream Dressing

½ *cup sour cream*
¼ *cup mayonnaise*
1 *teaspoon lemon juice*
½ *teaspoon sugar*
¼ *teaspoon dry mustard*
¼ *teaspoon onion juice*

Blend cream with remaining ingredients.

"Garlicy" Mayonnaise

2 *cloves garlic*
1 *cup mayonnaise*
1 *tablespoon olive oil*
1 *tablespoon lemon juice*

Peel garlic and crush in mixing bowl. Add mayonnaise, olive oil and lemon juice. The longer it stands the stronger it becomes!

Horseradish Sauce

1 *tablespoon chopped onion*
2 *tablespoons butter*
1 *tablespoon flour*
¾ *cup light cream*
¼ *cup prepared horse-radish*

Sauté onion in butter until lightly browned. Add flour; when bubbly, stir in cream. Cook, stirring, until sauce begins to thicken. Remove from heat. Stir in horseradish. Add salt to taste.

Spread warm on hamburger rolls, or chill and serve as dressing for salad.

Sauce may be stored, covered, in refrigerator one week or frozen, well wrapped, one month or a little longer.

Basic French Dressing

1 *teaspoon salt*	1 *teaspoon powdered*
½ *teaspoon coarse*	*sugar*
ground black pepper	¼ *cup vinegar*
½ *teaspoon paprika*	¾ *cup salad oil*

Mix dry ingredients with vinegar. Add oil, blend with wire wisk or fork.

Add if desired: One lightly beaten egg yolk before adding oil. Makes a thicker dressing.

Substitute lemon juice for vinegar.

Substitute one tablespoon dry sherry for one tablespoon of the vinegar. Add a few grains of cayenne, ½ teaspoon of dry mustard or herbs to taste.

Makes one cup

BARBECUE SAUCES

CHILI-HORSERADISH
SAUCE-ON-THE-MEAT

½ *cup chili sauce**	1 *tablespoon minced*
¼ *cup prepared horse-*	*onion*
radish	

Blend ingredients. Grill burger patty on one side, turn and top with a generous amount of the mixture while the other side cooks.

* *See page 77.*

EASY BARBECUE SAUCE

1 teaspoon prepared
mustard
1 tablespoon wine vine-
gar
4 tablespoons ketchup

2 cups semi-sweet sherry
4 tablespoons butter
¼ teaspoon salt
½ teaspoon pepper

Mix mustard with vinegar. Stir in remaining ingredients. Heat in heavy saucepan on barbecue grill. Use
to baste meat while grilling; spoon over cooked meat.

RED WINE BARBECUE SAUCE

⅓ cup red wine vinegar
2 tablespoons sugar
1 tablespoon prepared
mustard
1 teaspoon coarse ground
black pepper
1 teaspoon salt
6-8 drops Tabasco sauce

1 lemon sliced thin
1 medium size Bermuda
onion sliced thin
4 tablespoons butter
2 tablespoons Worcester-
shire sauce
1 cup dry red wine

Combine first ten ingredients in saucepan. Allow to
simmer over very low heat ten to fifteen minutes. Add
wine, cook ½ minute longer. Makes about two cups of
sauce.

TEXAS BARBECUE SAUCE

½ cup ketchup
¼ cup tarragon vinegar
2 tablespoons brown
sugar
1 teaspoon chili powder
⅛ teaspoon salt
1 clove garlic

1 bay leaf
1 stalk celery chopped
2 large ripe tomatoes
chopped
4 tablespoons butter
1 teaspoon paprika
½ teaspoon black pepper

Combine all ingredients in saucepan, bring to boil; lower heat, let barely simmer for fifteen minutes. Strain. Refrigerate, covered, until ready to use. Reheat in heavy saucepan on barbecue grill. Use to brush meat while grilling and to spoon over cooked meat.

Makes about two cups sauce or enough for two dozen hamburgers, plus a few more.

DRY BARBECUE SAUCE

3 tablespoons salt
2 tablespoons sugar
1 tablespoon paprika

1 tablespoon Beau Mondé seasoning
1 tablespoon coarse ground black pepper

Combine ingredients, mix well. Sprinkle liberally over meat before and during grilling.

CHILI SAUCE

½ pound ground beef
2 tablespoons beef suet
1 small onion
1 clove garlic
1 tablespoon chili pow-der (more or less as desired)
¼ teaspoon salt or to taste

¼ teaspoon ground cum-min seed
3 cups fresh chopped to-matoes
¾ cup water
¼ cup blended whiskey
2 tablespoons ketchup
1 teaspoon corn meal
1 teaspoon flour

Peel and chop onion, peel and mince garlic. Brown beef with suet, onion and garlic in saucepan. Add chili powder, salt, cummin, tomatoes (canned tomatoes may be substituted) and whiskey. Simmer gently over low heat for thrity minutes. Mix together ketchup, corn meal and flour. Stir into sauce. Cook, stirring until thickened.

Store in refrigerator one week or longer or freeze, well sealed. Use as needed.

EASY GOURMET TOMATO SAUCE

1 *small onion chopped*
1 *small green pepper chopped*
1 *tablespoon olive oil*
1 *tablespoon butter*
1 *teaspoon flour*

1 *(1 pound) can tomatoes or 1¾ cup stewed fresh tomatoes*
1 *bay leaf*
8 *peppercorns*
1 *tablespoon sugar*
½ *cup dry red wine*

Sauté onions and green pepper in oil and butter in a saucepan until limp but not browned. Stir in flour; when bubbly, add remaining ingredients. Blend. Simmer gently for twenty minutes. Strain if desired. Makes about two cups of sauce.

MARINARA SAUCE

1 *cup homemade or 1 (8 ounce) can tomato sauce*
¼ *teaspoon orégano*
½ *tablespoon minced parsley*
½ *minced clove garlic*
1 *tablespoon instant minced onion*

1 *tablespoon olive oil*
1 *tablespoon sugar*
2 *tablespoons tomato paste*
Salt
Coarse ground black pepper

Combine ingredients in saucepan. Allow to simmer gently until flavors blend (about ten minutes). Season to taste with salt and pepper. Makes about one and one-quarter cups sauce.

PIZZA SAUCE

¼ pound Italian sausage (chopped)
1 tablespoon olive oil
1 (#2) can Italian style tomatoes with basil
½ cup water
1 minced clove garlic
1 tablespoon minced onion
1 small can tomato paste
Salt
Coarse ground black pepper

Cook sausage in olive oil in saucepan until browned. Add remaining ingredients. Simmer gently for fifteen minutes. Makes about two cups sauce.

SAUCES TO POUR OVER

Dublin Butter Sauce

4 tablespoons softened butter
4 tablespoons ketchup
Salt
Pepper

Place butter and ketchup in skillet and stir until well blended. Cook over medium heat just until bubbly, do not allow to boil. Season to taste with salt and pepper. Pour over meat.

Mustard Butter Sauce

4 tablespoons butter
2 tablespoons Dijon mustard

Melt butter in skillet. Cook over medium flame until well heated, but do not allow to brown. Remove from heat, stir in mustard. Pour over meat.

Devil Sauce

2 tablespoons butter
1 tablespoon Worcester-
shire sauce
2 tablespoons ketchup
⅛ teaspoon garlic salt
1 tablespoon prepared
mustard

1 tablespoon chopped
chives
1 tablespoon chopped
parsley

Melt butter in skillet. Stir in remaining ingredients.
Heat thoroughly. Pour over meat.

Parsley Butter Sauce

3 tablespoons butter
2 tablespoons lemon juice
2 tablespoons chopped
parsley

Salt
Pepper

Melt butter in skillet. Cook until lightly browned; add
lemon and parsley. Cook, stirring, a few seconds longer.
Season to taste with salt and pepper. Pour over meat.

Sherry Mushroom Sauce

3 tablespoons butter
4-6 large fresh mushrooms
2 tablespoons dry sherry

Salt
Pepper

Chop mushrooms. Melt butter in skillet, add mushrooms. Cook, stirring frequently, one to two minutes.
Stir in sherry, add salt and pepper to taste. Cook,
stirring, a few seconds longer. Pour over meat.

Cheese and Beer Sauce

1 tablespoon butter
⅓ cup grated Monterey
  Jack Cheese
¾ cup beer

½ teaspoon Worcester-
  shire sauce
¼ teaspoon salt
¼ teaspoon dry mustard
Dash of cayenne pepper

Combine all ingredients in skillet. Cook, stirring, over medium heat until cheese is melted and sauce is bubbly hot. Pour over meat.

Tomato Cheese Sauce

1 tablespoon butter
1 teaspoon flour
¾ cup milk
⅓ cup grated sharp
  Cheddar cheese

1 tablespoon tomato
  paste
Salt
Pepper

Melt butter in skillet, stir in flour; when bubbly add milk. Cook, stirring, over low heat until sauce begins to thicken. Add cheese. Stir until cheese is melted. Add tomato paste and stir until well blended. Season with salt and pepper to taste. Pour over meat.

Olive Sauce

2 tablespoons butter
1 tablespoon finely
  chopped onion
1 tablespoon finely
  chopped green pepper
1 scant teaspoon flour

¾ cup dry red wine
¼ cup chopped green
  olives
Salt
Pepper

Melt butter in skillet, add chopped onion and green pepper. Cook over medium heat until vegetables are limp. Sprinkle with flour. Cook, stirring, until flour is lightly browned. Add wine, stir to blend. Cook over high heat until reduced about one third, add olives. Season with salt and pepper to taste and pour over meat.

Sauce à la Creme

4-6 shallots	*1 tablespoon Dijon*
1 tablespoon butter	*mustard*
2 tablespoons brandy	*Salt*
¾ cup heavy cream	*Pepper*

Peel and coarsely chop shallots, sauté in butter in skillet over medium heat until limp but not browned. Warm brandy, then add to shallots and ignite. Allow flame to burn out. Pour in cream. Cook, stirring frequently, five to six minutes. Remove from heat, stir in mustard, season to taste with salt and pepper. Pour over meat.

Anchovy Brown Sauce

2 tablespoons butter	*½ cup beef stock or*
1 teaspoon flour	*broth*
1 tablespoon minced	*1 teaspoon anchovy paste*
onion	*Pepper*

Melt butter in skillet. Stir in flour; when mixture is bubbly, add onions and stir until lightly browned. Add beet stock or broth. Cook, stirring, until sauce begins to thicken. Add anchovy paste, stir until well blended. Add pepper to taste. Pour over meat.

BUTTERS

Garlic Dill Butter

1 clove garlic
4 tablespoons butter
½ tablespoon dill weed
1 tablespoon lemon juice

½ teaspoon coarse
ground black pepper
⅛ teaspoon salt

Peel and mince garlic. Crush dill weed if dried or mince if fresh. Combine with butter and remaining ingredients. Cream until smooth.

Parsley Butter

4 tablespoons butter
2 tablespoons finely
chopped parsley

1 tablespoon lemon juice
⅛ teaspoon salt
⅛ teaspoon pepper

Combine all ingredients. Cream until smooth.

Roquefort Butter

3 tablespoons Roquefort
cheese
2 tablespoons butter

2 tablespoons heavy
cream

Crumble cheese, cream until smooth with butter and cream.

Fresh Tomato Butter

1 large ripe tomato
4-6 drops Tabasco sauce
½ teaspoon paprika
1 teaspoon olive oil

3 tablespoons butter
¼ teaspoon salt
¼ teaspoon coarse
ground black pepper

Plunge tomato into boiling water for a half minute, rinse under cold water, slip off skin, chop coarsely.

Cook in saucepan over medium heat until reduced to a thick pulp. Stir often, chop up large pieces with tip of spatula. Remove pan from heat, stir in Tabasco sauce, paprika and olive oil. Transfer to mixing bowl. Cool thoroughly, add butter, salt and pepper. Cream, then beat with fork until light and fluffy.

Peanut Butter Bacon Butter

2 tablespoons butter
2 tablespoons peanut but-
   ter
2 slices crisp-cooked
   bacon

½ teaspoon Worcester-
   shire sauce
¼ teaspoon pepper
Salt

Cream butter with peanut butter. Crumble bacon, stir in with Worcestershire sauce, pepper and salt to taste (depending on saltiness of bacon). Beat with wire whisk or fork until light.

Buttered Sauce Robért

3 tablespoons butter
1 tablespoon Sauce
   Robért (bottled)

1 teaspoon lemon juice
¼ teaspoon black pepper
¼ teaspoon salt

Combine ingredients. Cream together, then beat with fork or wire wisk until light.

Horseradish Butter

2 tablespoons butter
1 tablespoon prepared
   horseradish

2 tablespoons heavy
   cream
1 teaspoon prepared
   mustard

Combine ingredients, cream together, then beat with fork or wire whisk until light.

Garlic Butter

2 cloves garlic
3 tablespoons butter

2 tablespoons heavy
  cream
⅛ teaspoon salt

Peel garlic, mince fine. Combine with butter, cream and salt. Cream until smooth, beat with fork or wire whisk until light.

Curried Chutney Butter

3 tablespoons butter
2 tablespoons chutney

Pinch of curry powder

Chop chutney fine. Combine ingredients. Cream until smooth, then beat with fork or wire whisk until light.

Anchovy Butter

1 tablespoon anchovy
  paste

3 tablespoons butter
1 tablespoon heavy cream

Combine ingredients. Cream together, then beat with fork or wire whisk until light.

Parmesan Butter

2 tablespoons grated Par-
  mesan cheese

3 tablespoons butter
2-3 dashes Tabasco sauce

Combine ingredients. Cream until smooth, beat with wire whisk or fork until light.

Herb Butter

¼ teaspoon dried flaked
  parsley
¼ teaspoon thyme
¼ teaspoon sweet basil

¼ teaspoon dried onion
  flakes
1 tablespoon olive oil
4 tablespoons butter
¼ teaspoon salt

Place herbs in small bowl, add olive oil. Let stand at room temperature one hour or longer. Add butter. Cream until smooth, then beat with fork or wire whisk until light.

Note: All butters are sufficient for four to six hamburgers.

6

All American Star-Spangled Parties, Menus and Meals

Great parties are made up of congenial people, pleasant surroundings, good food, good drink and a relaxed unhurried, unharried hostess or host.

Hamburger menus meet the requirements—everyone likes them—the party giver is relaxed, because, good as they are, hamburger meals are always simple and with a little preplanning, easy to prepare. No need to be hurried or harried. Good food makes for congeniality and congeniality makes surroundings seem pleasant, no matter if simple or grand.

Texas Burger Barbecue

Big party—small house? Plan it for the great outdoors.

Hamburgers
with Texas Barbecue Sauce
Corn Chips
Texas Tomato and Cucumber Salad
Western Baked Beans   Guacamole Salad
Beer   Cokes

87

Southern Ambrosia
"Easy to Eat" Cake Squares
Coffee

Tips: Some things you need for barbecuing hamburgers are portable charcoal brazier, grill or outdoor fireplace with grate. Charcoal, charcoal briquettes or seasoned wood. Long handled skillet for barbecue sauce, brush for basting, asbestos gloves.

"Make aheads" include: *Baked beans* (page 68); reheat in outdoor Dutch oven or on grill. *Barbecue sauce* (page 76); reheat on grill. *Tomato and cucumber salad* (page 73); store in refrigerator on long platter, well covered and sealed with plastic wrap or foil. *Ambrosia*; equal parts of grapefruit sections, orange sections and coconut (actually better for waiting, so make it the night before). *Cake squares*; buy from a baker or make your own a day, a week or a month in advance; cut, wrap and store in freezing compartment of refrigerator or home freezer. *Guacamole* (page 70); contrary to popular opinion, it can also be prepared in advance; however, it is best if made as close to serving time as possible.

What's left to do? Start the fire two or three hours before guests are due to arrive. Set the table, get ready for the party yourself (blue jeans and western shirt are appropriate gear), then bring out the food. Party's begun!

Everybody's Birthday Party
For Kids of All Ages

Birthday Hamburgers

Cheddar Cheese Burgers
for "seconds"
Potato chips   Bread and Butter Pickles
Cokes   Milk
Ice Cream   and   Birthday Cake

Tips: Set a real "old fashioned" birthday table with
party snappers, paper hats and souvenirs. Use the
birthday cake as a centerpiece. Serve plain hamburgers with a birthday candle in the center of each.
Bring hamburgers to the table on a large platter each
one with its candle lighted. If possible, have the dining
room lights dimmed for a moment. We've yet to see
anyone of any age who didn't delight in a flaming
dish—especially of their favorite food!

Cocktail "Cook In" (Or Out)

Sophisticated finger food to go with drinks—great tasting—but easy to prepare for four or forty.

Miniature Cocktail Burgers
with an Assortment of
"Butters Plus"
Dill Pickle Slices   Ripe Olives
Potato Sticks
Icy Bowl of "Crisp-cooked" and Raw Vegetables with
Roquefort Dip
Martinis   Scotch and Soda
Miniature French Pastries
Coffee

Tips: You will need an electric skillet or a chafing dish
to keep burger patties hot while serving. However,
absolutely everything can be prepared in advance of

your party. Pan fry bite size meat patties to very rare, brown on the outside, pink to red within. One pound meat will make about twenty miniature patties. Plan on serving four to six per person. Cover and keep on the back of the stove. When ready to serve, transfer to electric skillet or chafing dish; reheat and keep warm in a generous amount of butter. If it's a large party, have refills waiting in the kitchen. Serve on miniature hamburger rolls. If these are not available in your community, make them yourself from large hamburger rolls: use miniature cookie cutter to cut two or three small rolls from one large one.

For ice bowl of crisp-cooked and raw vegetables; place small amount of crushed ice in a large bowl; (silver, silver plated or stainless steel bowls are best). Place a slightly smaller bowl in the center. Pack crushed ice between the two bowls almost but not quite to the rim. Prepare an assortment of vegetables: cauliflower flowerets, celery hearts, turnip sticks, firm, small hearts of lettuce, carrot fingers, radish roses, scallions and strips of green pepper. Fill bowl with vegetables, bring to cocktail buffet table on silver or stainless steel platter. Have cocktail picks nearby for spearing vegetables and dunking in dip.

Crisp-cook and raw vegetables: cook bite-size cauliflower flowerets and carrot fingers separately in salted water to just cover for three to four minutes. Drain. Marinate in oil and vinegar dressing one to two hours. Drain and combine with raw celery, radishes, lettuce, scallions, green pepper and turnip slices. Toss well with a small amount of Basic French dressing (page 75). Season with salt and pepper.

Roquefort Dip: One part Roquefort cheese to two

parts cottage cheese. Blend in electric blender until smooth and fluffy. Or cream together, then whip with a wire wisk.

If you do not have a sufficiently large table to accommodate your entire cocktail buffet menu, use three or four small tables scattered around the room. A hamburger table with meat patties in electric skillet or chafing dish; miniature rolls, preferably in a bun warmer; three or four bowls of "Butters Plus" (pages 44–45) and small plates for serving. A second table can hold the vegetable bowl and dip bowl and potato sticks; another, scotch, soda, ice and the "makings" for Martinis. And a table for dessert and coffee, the best drink for that "one for the road."

"After the Party" Party For Midnight or Later

Sicilian Joe Burgers
Salad of "Everything Green"
Chianti Wine
Fresh Pineapple with Kirsch
Chocolate Mints
Espresso

Tips: This is a party to come home to after a night on the town. Almost everything can be prepared in advance. Salad preparation comes early in the day— washing, separating leaves, tearing (not cutting) into bite size. Use endive, escarole, bib lettuce, romaine, fresh young spinach leaves, etc. Store in refrigerator in plastic bags. Prepare Basic French dressing (page 75) or Sour Cream Dressing (page 74) and toss with salad just before serving.

The filling for Sicilian Joe Burgers (page 52) is made next. Store, well covered, in the same skillet in which it was cooked. Prepare rolls, wrap in foil.

Prepare pineapple: peel, core and cube, sprinkle with Kirsch. Set your table and there you are—nothing left to do when you return home with your guests but open the wine, reheat the meat mixture, assemble and broil the burgers, start the coffee—and—midnight supper is served!

Bridge Lunch for the Girls

Elegance is what's needed here, but what could be more elegant than:

Icy Tomato-orange Soup
Dutchess Burgers
Rosé Wine
Fresh Fruit Compote Grand Marnier
Crisp Cookies
Coffee

Tips: Serve soup in living room in well chilled pottery mugs. Make soup by mixing canned tomato soup and fresh orange juice, half and half, with a dash of Tabasco Sauce; chill in refrigerator, and just before serving, decorate each icy cold serving with a sprig of mint.

Bring Duchess Burgers (page 48) to the table after guests are seated; they make impressive plates.

Chill the wine in a traditional wine bucket, placed near you to pour after you are seated—more festive that way.

Prepare compote of whatever fresh fruit is in season:

ripe peaches, orange slices, pitted fresh cherries, fresh pineapple fingers, green or purple grapes, etc. Add a generous jigger of Grand Marnier liqueur for each four servings and let fruit mellow, well covered with plastic wrap or foil, two or three hours before serving.

Burger Buffet

A "help yourself" young party—a fun party for host and hostess as well as for guests.

Choice of
Rabbit Burgers
or
Plain Hamburgers
Platter of tomato slices, avocado slices, onion rings
Relish tray
Salad Bowl
Ketchup   Chili sauce
Potato Salad
Beer   Cokes   Red wine

Tips: You will need a "chef" for the Rabbit burgers (page 14) and Ham-burgers (page 25). Give this job to one of your male friends; he'll love it—do it yourself only if you must. It's best at any party to be free to circulate among your guests. As with all hamburger parties you can because almost everything is prepared in advance.

Prepare meat patties and bring to the cooking table on a long platter. Place conveniently near the electric skillet or grill. Have the Welsh Rabbit warming in a chafing dish close at hand. Split and wrap buns loosely in foil. Seal edges, heat in medium oven (350°). Bring wrapped to table. Unwrap only when ready to assemble burgers. Have "seconds" wrapped and ready to heat.

Arrange tomato and avocado slices with onion rings on a platter, sprinkle with chopped parsley. Pour Basic French Dressing (substitute lemon juice for the vinegar) over all and allow to marinate in refrigerator for an hour.

Prepare a relish tray of cucumber pickles, mustard pickles, chopped onion, radish roses and pimento-stuffed green olives.

Use torn crisp lettuce and raw spinach leaves for the salad bowl; decorate with cherry tomatoes and have a bowl of Sour Cream Dressing (page 74) on the side.

Make sure the ketchup and chili sauce are at room temperature, but have the potato salad icy cold.

Beer and cokes: Put them in a large ice-filled wooden bucket and let everyone help themselves. Have four or five bottle openers available—they do have a way of getting misplaced!

Index

95